Health Technical Memorandum 2015

Management policy

Bedhead services

London: HMSO

NHS Estates

An Executive Agency of the Department of Health

HMSO
Standing order service

Placing a standing order with HMSO BOOKS enables a
customer to receive future titles in this series automatically
as published. This saves the time, trouble and expense of
placing individual orders and avoids the problem of
knowing when to do so. For details please write to HMSO
BOOKS (PC 13A/1), Publications Centre, PO Box 276,
London SW8 5DT quoting reference 14 02 017.
The standing order service also enables customers to
receive automatically as published all material of their
choice which additionally saves extensive catalogue
research. The scope and selectivity of the service has been
extended by new techniques, and there are more than
3,500 classifications to choose from. A special leaflet
describing the service in detail may be obtained on
request.

About this publication

Health Technical Memoranda (HTMs) give comprehensive advice and guidance on the design, installation and operation of specialised building and engineering technology used in the delivery of healthcare.

They are applicable to new and existing sites, and are for use at various stages during the inception, design, construction, refurbishment and maintenance of a building.

Health Technical Memorandum 2015

HTM 2015 (Bedhead services) focuses on:

- the legal, mandatory and functional requirements;

- design applications;

- maintenance of systems; and

- operation of systems

of electrical, communications and medical gases terminal units required at the bedhead and at other patient locations in all types of healthcare premises.

It is published as four separate volumes each addressing a specialist discipline:

- this volume – **Management policy** – outlines the overall responsibility of general managers/chief executives of healthcare premises and details their legal and mandatory obligations in providing adequate electrical/ communications and medical gas pipeline system facilities for patients. It summarises the technical aspects involved and concludes with a list of definitions;

- **Design considerations** – highlights the overall requirements and considerations that should be applied to the design up to the contract document;

- **Validation and verification** – details the requirements for ensuring that manufactured equipment is formally tested and certified as to contract and manufactured to the highest level of quality assurance. The importance of commissioning is emphasised and the order of tests on site is listed. Routine testing, which is a subset of these commissioning tests, is also reviewed;

- **Operational management** – provides guidance for those responsible for overseeing and operating day-to-day running and maintenance. Coverage includes voltage supplies, medical gas pipeline systems, instrumentation performance, quality of radio/television (TV) reception and alarm system function. Record keeping is also discussed.

Guidance in this Health Technical Memorandum is complemented by the library of National Health Service Model Engineering Specifications. Users of the guidance are advised to refer to the relevant specifications for:

a. medical gases;

b. common services electrical (low and extra-low);

c. nurse call systems.

The contents of this Health Technical Memorandum in terms of management policy, operational policy and technical guidance are endorsed by:

- the Welsh Office for the NHS in Wales;

- the Health and Personal Social Services Management Executive in Northern Ireland;

- the National Health Service in Scotland Management Executive

and set standards consistent with Departmental Cost Allowances.

References to legislation appearing in the main text of this document apply in England and Wales. Where references differ for Scotland and/or Northern Ireland these are given as marginal notes.

Where appropriate, marginal notes are also used to amplify the text.

Contents

1.0 Scope

The importance of achieving correct maintenance/service for complex equipment cannot be overstressed. Unless the management has complete confidence in the ability of the engineering staff to carry out adequate repairs and preventative maintenance, those functions should be assigned to the manufacturer or supplier.

1.1 Healthcare premises will achieve maximum efficacy when patients receive quality treatment appropriate to their needs with the minimum length of stay. To this end the services provided at the point of nursing, that is, at the bedhead, should be tailored to meet not only the short term requirements but also the longer term.

1.2 The degree of sophistication will vary greatly over the range between low dependency areas such as geriatric assessment, and intensive care wards.

1.3 The degree of engineering necessary to provide the nominated services will be influenced by the building structure. Supporting equipment in lightweight walling consisting of composite partitioning will require a totally different approach to established solid walling with possible deep window recesses.

Refer to HTM 2014 – 'Abatement of electrical interference'.

1.4 When microprocessors are used in alarm and control systems associated with the patient, this demands strict attention by both supplier and site management, to prevent potential problems with electrostatic discharges (ESD) derived from the high static voltages capable of being generated at the bedside. All electrical goods will need to comply with current legislation dealing with electromagnetic compatibility (EMC).

2.0 Management responsibilities

Statutory requirements and functional guidance

2.1 It is the responsibility of general managers/chief executives to ensure that their premises comply with all statutes.

2.2 Managers (owners or occupiers) of healthcare premises have an overriding general duty of care under the Health and Safety at Work etc Act 1974 (the HSW Act 1974).

Health and Safety at Work (Northern Ireland) Order 1978

2.3 Electrical supplies, manufactured equipment and work practices should comply with the following legislation and guidance in total or in part as applicable:

  a. the electricity act 1989[1];

  b. the Electricity Supply Regulations, 1988 (as amended 1992)[2];

  c. the Electricity at Work Regulations 1989[3];

  d. the Safety Signs Regulations 1980[4];

  e. BS7671: 1992 the Requirements for Wiring Installations (the IEE Wiring Regulations, 16th Edition);

  f. the Electromagnetic Compatibility Regulations 1992[5];

  g. HTM 2011 – 'Emergency electrical services';

  h. HTM 2007 – 'Electrical services: supply and distribution';

  j. HTM 2014 – 'Abatement of electrical interference';

  k. The lighting guide – Hospitals and Health Care Buildings (LG2: CIBSE);

  m. HTM 2020 – 'Electrical safety code for low voltage systems'.

[1]The Electricity Act 1989 (Modification of Local Enactment) Scotland Order 1990. Electricity (Northern Ireland) Order 1992.

[2]Electricity Supply Regulations (Northern Ireland) 1991. (as amended 1993)

[3]Electricity at Work Regulations (Northern Ireland) 1991.

[4]Safety Signs Regulations (Northern Ireland) 1981.

[5]Implementing EC Directive on Electromagnetic Compatibility (89/336/EEC).

Other obligations

2.4 Management have broader obligations to ensure that where facilities derive power from essential electrical supplies, these supplies are maintained during any short or long term interruptions in the normal supply. See HTM 2011 – 'Emergency electrical services'.

2.5 Where bedhead services include medical gas pipeline systems, the design and maintenance of these will need to comply with HTM 2022 – 'Medical gas pipeline systems'.

Functional requirements

2.6 The following is a typical list of bedhead services, at least some of which will usually be required at any patient bed position; however, the list is not exhaustive:

  a. patient to staff calling device;

  b. staff to staff calling device (emergency);

  c. entertainment;

    d. medical gas pipeline system;

    e. mains power supplies;

    f. telephone outlet;

    g. patient monitoring apparatus;

    h. lighting for ward/patient reading;

    j. patient to nurse speech communication;

    k. computer outlet (patient-data);

    m. nurse to nurse speech communication;

    n. cardiac alarm.

2.7 In areas away from the bed, equipment associated with the bedhead services will be required, typically:

    a. nurse station or staff base – indicators, sounders, controls;

    b. treatment rooms, day-spaces, physiotherapy, hydrotherapy, toilets, bathrooms – calling and reset facilities;

    c. corridors, utility rooms, kitchen, sluice etc – tone sounders and repeat indicator lights;

    d. engineers department – central radio/TV programme generation equipment;

    e. laundry/workshops – entertainment loudspeakers/control units.

Operational management

2.8 Management should ensure that an operational plan is in place for each site under their control. This should comprise:

    a. a list and description of the main emergency plant and electrical equipment associated with the 240 V supply;

    b. a list showing the location of essential medical gas supply equipment such as plant and local area control valves;

    c. identification of qualified personnel with adequate training given by supplier;

    d. a schedule of maintenance dates for each class of equipment, and where maintenance is contracted out, details of contractors including call-out telephone numbers;

    e. a control system to monitor performance against the maintenance plan;

    f. an inventory of spare parts stock;

    g. a schedule of possible emergency incidents with remedial operational procedures;

    h. a routine of staff training in the operation of the various bedhead services.

Designated staff functions

2.9 Only trained, authorised and competent persons should be appointed by management to control the operation of emergency services and to service/maintain the elements of bedhead services.

2.10 Management – the owner, occupier, employer, general manager, chief executive or other person who is accountable for the premises and is responsible for issuing or implementing a general policy statement under the HSW Act 1974.

2.11 Designated person (electrical: low voltage) – the person who has overall authority and responsibility for the premises containing the low voltage electrical systems within the premises, and with a duty under the HSW Act 1974 to prepare and issue a general policy statement on health and safety at work including the organisation and arrangements for carrying out that policy. This person should not be the authorising engineer.

2.12 Duty holder – the person on whom the Electricity at Work Regulations 1989 impose a duty in connection with safety.

2.13 Authorising engineer (electrical: low voltage) – a chartered engineer with appropriate experience or an incorporated electrical engineer, possessing the necessary degree of independence from local management, who is appointed in writing by the management to implement, administer and monitor the safety arrangements for the low voltage electrical supply and distribution systems of the premises, to ensure compliance with the Electricity at Work Regulations 1989 and to assess the suitability and appointment of candidates in writing to be "authorised persons – electrical: low voltage" (see HTM 2020 – 'Electrical safety code for low voltage systems').

2.14 Authorised person (electrical: low voltage) – an individual possessing adequate technical knowledge and having received appropriate training, appointed in writing by the authorising engineer to be responsible for the practical implementation and operation of management's safety policy and procedures on defined electrical systems (see HTM 2020).

2.15 Competent person (electrical: low voltage) – an individual who, in the opinion of an authorised person, has sufficient technical knowledge and experience to prevent danger while carrying out work on defined electrical systems.

2.16 Authorised person (medical gas pipeline systems – MGPS) – a person who has sufficient technical knowledge, training and experience to enable him/her to understand fully the dangers involved and who is appointed in writing by management on the recommendation of a chartered engineer with specialist knowledge of MGPS (refer to HTM 2022 – 'Medical gas pipeline systems').

2.17 Competent person (MGPS) – a person having sufficient knowledge and experience to enable him/her to carry out his/her duties in a competent manner and who understands fully the dangers involved and whose name is on the register of competent persons (MPGS) (refer to HTM 2022 – 'Medical gas pipeline systems').

Definitions

2.18 Injury – death or personal injury from electric shock, electrical burn, electrical explosion or arcing, or from fire/explosion initiated by electrical energy or misuse/faults with medical gas supplies.

2.19 System – a system in which all the electrical equipment is, or may be, electrically connected to a common source of electrical energy, including such source and such equipment.

This definition for low voltage incorporates the extra low voltage (ELV) range as defined in the IEE Wiring Regulations

2.20   Low voltage (LV) – the existence of a potential difference (rms value for a.c.) normally not exceeding 1000 volts a.c. or 1500 volts d.c. between circuit conductors or 600 volts a.c. or 900 volts d.c. between circuit conductors and earth.

2.21   System (communication) – a system designed to provide transfer of information between two or more locations, either by direct wiring or by other means. The system will embrace the necessary control units and power supplies.

2.22   System (medical gas pipeline) – a system designed to provide medical gases, medical compressed air and vacuum, derived from plant room, compound and/or manifold rooms and including all associated peripheral equipment such as regulators, area valves, alarm and control systems.

2.23   Essential circuits – circuits forming part of the essential services electrical supply so arranged that they can be supplied separately from the remainder of the electrical installation.

2.24   Bedhead service – a facility provided for patient and/or staff to enable the carrying out of medical and surgical functions and entertainment, comprising of a fixed installation behind or to the side of the bed but also embracing other areas of the ward or establishment to which or from which the bedhead service is connected for the purpose of support.

3.0 Functional overview

Types of installation

3.1 This document is applicable primarily to new hospitals and major refurbishment work but the principles also apply to alterations and extensions to existing installations.

3.2 The rapid increase in demand for healthcare premises offering advanced surgical and medical care has led to a proportional increase in demand for enhanced facilities at the patient/nurse interface, for example bed, day space, treatment room, toilets.

3.3 The design of the bedhead services installation should, as far as possible, be ergonomically sound. Facilities that are difficult to use tend to be not used or wrongly used. Good accessibility is important for both the nurse and the patient.

3.4 Maintenance on some parts of the bedhead services installation may have to be on a regular basis, for example medical gas terminal units. All equipment should be afforded adequate access for maintenance to minimise downtime and disruption. Where extra cost put into the installation initially can be seen to achieve reduced maintenance effort or time, then this should be given due consideration.

3.5 Conventionally, extra low voltage (ELV) services to the bedhead can be supplied by hard wire systems using individual cables or on data cable using digital technology.

3.6 The electrical installation within the healthcare premises should be designed to minimise interruptions in the supply due to internal faults.

3.7 Modern electronic equipment will normally incorporate internal battery back-up supplies to maintain essential memory functions. It is nevertheless good practice to connect nurse call and similar systems to the emergency electrical services.

3.8 Where piped medical gas is provided at the bedhead, the gas installation may be separate or incorporated in the physical enclosures associated with the electrical services. In all cases the requirements of HTM 2022 – 'Medical gas pipeline systems' should be observed.

3.9 Typical means of installing the medical gas pipeline system and/or the electrical services to the bedhead will take one or more of the following methods:

  a. separate pipes and conduit tubes set into the wall structure and terminating in flush wall boxes housing the electrical service or gas terminal unit. The direction of travel is usually vertically from the ceiling voids;

It is normally the case that this method will only apply to new premises or major refurbishment of existing buildings.

b. proprietary trunking surface fixed horizontally along the wall behind the bedhead. All electrical services and gas pipes can be accommodated together. Connection will still be made to the ceiling void either by conduits and pipes at the end of the horizontal run or by a vertical section of the trunking usually at the end of the horizontal run, or if necessary, part way along. The length of horizontal run is unlimited within reason and could embrace the length of several wards;

Also refer to ITU solutions in HBN 27.

c. proprietary trunking surface fixed vertically to bring all services down to the bedhead from the ceiling void.

3.10 Trunking systems can be justified, in terms of costs, where:

- there are a large number of services required at the bed;

- wards are being upgraded and the existing building structure cannot be adapted to house concealed pipes and conduits;

- walls consist of relatively lightweight material such as composite partitioning sometimes with a glazed upper half;

- easy access may be required in the future for equipment modification or additional facilities;

- the resulting service penetration of the wall partition could impair the fire compartmentation requirements.

3.11 The practice of mounting bedhead services within moveable lockers with a flexible connection to the wall is not recommended.

3.12 Where fixed lockers are positioned to the side of the bed and take up the full height between floor and ceiling, then it may be deemed preferable to flush mount all or some of the electrical services (not medical gas) into the side of the locker facing the patient.

3.13 In the majority of cases, a nurse will treat the patient from the right hand side. The facilities therefore should where practical be positioned on that side. In some cases treatment is required from the patient's left; the equipment should not be obscured if the bed or furniture is moved to allow treatment from that side. In critical cases, provision for treatment from either side is required.

3.14 Provision should be made to prevent the bed or bed attachments damaging the bedhead services equipment while the bed is being moved, raised or lowered.

Communication – patient/nurse

3.15 For some in-patient accommodation, it is argued that any method of calling for assistance is likely to be misused, for example by children and psychiatric patients. A basic form of nurse call system is nevertheless arguable since this will provide flexibility for the future and if the appropriate calling device is specified, it can be detached as inoperable.

3.16 It is not practical to expect bedded patients to operate controls from a wall mounted panel, and the use of hand held units is a universal practice. Connection to the wall panel should be by an ultra-flexible lightweight cable and a plug which will easily disengage if strain is applied to the cable. The range of hand held control units varies from a simple call push with or without reassurance light, to a sophisticated multi-function handset to provide nurse call, radio/TV sound selection and volume control, bedlight switching and speech intercommunication. A means of attaching the control unit to the bedclothes or patient's clothes should be provided, and also a means of storing the unit on the wall or bedside furniture when not in use.

3.17 It is possible to provide a dual function arrangement whereby the entertainment channels and volume controls can be duplicated on the wall panel for selection and control by the nurse when patients are too incapacitated to operate them.

3.18 In areas such as a dayspace, it is usually sufficient to provide a wall mounted push button for nurse call. In bathrooms, showers and toilets, a pull cord switch is preferred, or as an alternative a suitably rated waterproof wall mounted call push.

3.19 In response to a patient making a call, if following "follow the light principle", lamps should be illuminated steadily: at the calling point outside the ward, at the nurse station and at any other necessary locations, for example the sister's office. The lamp at the calling point should be specific to the patient: other lamps may be provided for a group of calling points, for example a multi-bed ward. Other methods, for example liquid crystal displays, LED boards or VDUs may also be used.

3.20 In addition to lamp indication of a call, an audible signal tone should be provided at strategic positions throughout the ward. The tone should sound intermittently 1 second on/9 seconds off until cancelled. If required, a quietening switch at the nurse station should be provided to subdue the tone at night.

3.21 For non-speech systems resetting of the call should be achieved at the calling point only – by operating a reset push button.

3.22 The addition of a speech facility to a nurse call system can save nursing time. It has the advantage that nursing staff at the staff base can ascertain the needs of the patient prior to attending the bed. It eliminates some visits altogether, yet still gives reassurance to the patient. The staff base indicator in a speech system should have an indicator to identify the source of each call.

Communication – staff/staff (emergency)

3.23 With the possible exception of low dependency areas, it is necessary to give nursing staff the ability to call for assistance should the need arise while attending to a patient. A switch for this purpose should be incorporated in the bedhead services panel and in any other area where assistance may be required. Areas which have no other form of communication may require this facility, for example treatment rooms. The switch will operate with a pull on/push off action to prevent inadvertent operation. It should be coloured red.

3.24 Use of an emergency switch should cause the patient call lamps (see paragraph 3.19) to illuminate in a flashing mode, that is, 0.5 seconds on/0.5 seconds off until the call is cancelled by returning the switch to normal.

3.25 Use of an emergency switch should cause the tone sounders to operate with dual tone sound in sympathy with the flashing lamps.

Entertainment

3.26 Entertainment for the patient is important for their wellbeing and is available in various forms and derived from:

    a. television (TV);

    b. radio;

    c. compact disc (CD) player;

    d. cassette tape player;

    e. video cassette recorder (VCR); and

    f. satellite (TV).

3.27 Larger healthcare establishments may wish to provide space for a central console to house the above facilities, and perhaps also a hospital radio station.

3.28 Where television is provided, the means of relaying the sound to the patient will depend on circumstances:

    a. a single-bed ward usually has a direct TV loudspeaker;

    b. a small multi-bed ward will either use the loudspeaker direct or will have the sound output of the TV wired around the bed positions for headphone listening, the room loudspeaker being disconnected. Alternatively, all TV programmes can be generated centrally for distribution around all wards;

    c. a large ward may have more than one TV set, so centrally generated programmes fed to headphones becomes the best solution;

    d. where centrally generated programmes are installed, all beds in all wards should be served by this equipment;

    e. there is obvious advantage in having silent TV monitors.

3.29 Technology has brought about dramatic changes in the way hospital multi-channel programme distribution takes place by using digital techniques. High quality sound channels can be generated from a central unit and transferred through data cable to all bedheads and decoded by the bedhead electronics. Selection and volume control is achieved via the handset or the controls on the bedhead.

Control of the TV picture will be by the remote control unit supplied with the TV or manually by patient or staff.

3.30 Where a loudspeaker is required in a non-bedded area, a loudspeaker control unit is connected to the distributing data cable and to a power supply.

Medical gas pipeline systems

3.31 Where medical gas pipeline systems are used, the terminal unit provided should be as indicated in the relevant Health Building Note, Activity Data Sheet, HTM 2022 and BS5682: 1987.

3.32 Methods of installation should be to HTM 2022 – 'Medical gas pipeline systems'.

3.33 Where terminal units are integrated with other bedhead services, care must be taken to ensure adequate space for ease of use of medical equipment such as flowmeters, vacuum control units etc.

Mains power supplies

3.34 At least one twin 13 amp switched socket-outlet should be provided at each bed position; it is convenient to incorporate the sockets along with other bedhead services. For an intensive care unit (ICU), the number of 13A switched sockets required could be as many as 24 or more. Where sockets are connected to the essential supply this needs to be made obvious, usually by specifying the switch rocker to be coloured red. Some departments may require the availability of a 2-pin shaver socket.

Lighting (bedhead luminaire)

3.35 Most bedhead installations should include a reading lamp which is fixed to the wall at high level, or lower down as part of the bedhead services equipment. In the latter case the fitting should be of the articulated adjustable type. Illumination, positioning and tilt restrictions should comply with the recommendations of the CIBSE Hospital and Health Care Buildings Lighting Guide (LG2) or BS4533, 102.55 and 103.2 whichever is appropriate.

3.36 The reading lamp can be provided as an integral part of a surface trunking system. Such luminaires should provide the required luminance allowing for the shielding of the patient's head and shoulders. Where such luminaires are installed in trunking along with medical gas pipeline systems, control of glare and convenience for the use of terminal units require careful positioning.

3.37 It is advisable to arrange for the reading lamp to be dimmed for night inspection. Control of the lamp can be by a two-way centre-off rocker switch providing dim-off-bright. In the bright position, the patient can have on-off control via a switch on the handset.

3.38 The use of compact fluorescent rather than GLS lamps is becoming universal; they should certainly be considered for the bedhead luminaires. Dimming of these is achieved by using a fitting with two lamps, typically one at 13 watts, the other at 5 watts, and switching from one to the other.

Telephones

3.39 Where a bedside telephone facility is required, this can be incorporated within the bedhead services wall panel and take one of two forms:

a. an individual standard telephone socket per bed wired as a separate extension to the hospital switchboard (this will allow the use of private telephones or simultaneous use of more than one mobile payphone);

b. an individual standard telephone socket per bed wired in parallel to other beds in the same ward on a common single circuit to the switchboard. A mobile payphone can be plugged in where required, but only one at a time.

Patient monitoring

3.40 In the high dependency areas where apparatus connected to a patient needs to be monitored remotely, the connection of the equipment can be accommodated by the bedhead services panel using special plugs and sockets and screened cables as necessary.

a. Current discussion on the introduction of a harmonised plug and socket system for Europe is likely to generate public resistance. No long term advice can be given at this stage.

b. All low voltage (240 V) supplies and accessories should be installed strictly to the current IEE Wiring Regulations (BS7671: 1992).

Your attention is drawn to DOH Safety Action Bulletin No. 69 where it is advised that luminaires should only be used for the purposes for which they are designed. Unprotected lamps used for examination purposes where splashes of liquid may occur can result in lamp explosion. Examination luminaires should be to the relevant British Standard.

Nurse presence

The success of a nurse presence system will depend on the discipline exercised in operating the switches for each and every visit.

3.41 A nurse presence system will provide a means of locating nursing staff within the total ward area. Each room and bay can be provided with a switch for the nurses to operate as they enter and leave the location. In single bed rooms the switch can be part of the bedhead services installation, but more usually it is placed at the entrance of each area so fitted. Operation of the switch will illuminate a lamp adjacent to or integral with the switch, a lamp over the door or in the corridor and a lamp for each location at the nurse station indicator. If required, a tone sounder in each area can be switched on by the presence switch to alert the nurse in the event of a patient call.

3.42 Where speech systems are installed it is usual for a presence facility to incorporate a ward loudspeaker microphone for each area covered by a presence switch to enable the nurse station to communicate with the nurse.

3.43 All speech systems associated with patients should be designed to ensure that no eavesdropping can take place. Where it may be necessary to monitor the sound from a bed position, any loss of privacy should be indicated to the patient for as long as the monitoring takes place.

Staff base

3.44 The staff base, or nurse station, is the administrative and communication centre of the ward. It is here that both visual and audible signals are received from patients and staff as well as monitoring information in the high dependency departments. A typical nurse station control unit might take the form of a console or a panel mounted into the desk or on the wall alongside and may include:

- the patient call indicator lamps;

- the nurse presence lamps;

- the audible alarm for patient and staff (emergency) calls;

- a sound attenuation switch for night use;

- where a speech system is installed, a loudspeaker and/or handset;

- a lamp and sounder operated by the "door bell" push situated at the ward entrance;

- an intruder alarm switch to raise an alarm within the ward and an adjacent ward, also possibly the hospital switchboard;

- a closed circuit TV where there is a high risk of undesirable intrusion at the ward entrance door; the provision of a television monitor with intercom facility can be a useful aid to staff security.

Transfer of calls

3.45 Where staff take on the responsibility for the adjacent ward or wards (for example during the night) it is advisable to incorporate a transfer system whereby any calls from the adjacent ward or wards are enunciated at the duty nurse station.

3.46 The geography of a floor layout may be such as to make practical a flexible nursing approach embracing two or more ward areas. Where the degree of patient dependency or bed occupancy varies greatly or regularly it will be advantageous to have the ability to expand or diminish the number of beds covered by the relative nurse stations. Modern nurse call systems can easily accommodate such manipulation.

Repeat indicator units

3.47 For occasions when the staff base is left unattended it is necessary to provide a master indicator with or without tone sounder in all areas where a member of staff may be, including utility rooms. The indicator will illuminate for all patient calls (steady) and all staff calls (flashing).

Cardiac alarm

3.48 If a cardiac alarm system is installed it should be initiated by a special protected switch at the bed position. The cardiac call should register at a permanently manned centre such as the switchboard which will alert the cardiac team via telephones or some other means.

Attack alarm

3.49 Staff have become vulnerable to attack in areas such as psychiatric wards and accident and emergency departments and it may be appropriate to provide an attack alarm system. A body-worn transmitting device can be activated by the wearer to alert, via a receiver unit or units, other members of staff. It is essential that the **location** of the attack can be readily ascertained.

4.0 Management action

4.1 It is the responsibility of management to ensure that patients and staff are provided with services at the bed and at other nursing locations to fulfil the clinical needs of that nursing location for as long as can be foreseen.

4.2 These services should be reassessed periodically by the management to ensure they remain adequate. The frequency will depend on the care provided.

4.3 To ensure that bedhead services installations remain adequate, safe and reliable, medical, nursing and administrative action is essential to introduce and enforce operational policies designed to minimise the dangers that may arise from misuse. Those policies should ensure that no work, however minor, can be undertaken without the knowledge and permission of the appropriate responsible officer.

4.4 Medical and technical staff should understand the generation and effects of electrostatic discharge.

4.5 Specifying over-complex equipment should be resisted. The electrical and medical gas pipeline systems should be kept simple and practicable while being fit for purpose.

4.6 While non-essential bedhead services such as entertainment may be seen as low priority, where these are installed it is important that they function to help maintain morale and avoid frustration in the patient. An entertainment service which is of poor quality or even inoperable will be particularly dispiriting.

4.7 All suppliers of equipment and services should be quality assured to at least BS5750/EN29000/ISO9000.

4.8 The specifiers of complex equipment should satisfy themselves that the suppliers of the equipment are organisations of sufficient substance to maintain the equipment.

4.9 Before management specify a nurse call system, consideration should be given to whether the communications within the ward are to be controlled locally or centrally.

4.10 Modern technology makes viable the opportunity to oversee all alarm systems at a central console showing patient calls, staff calls (emergency), nurse locations (presence system) etc. These, along with a speech link to the wards and visual display units, can provide an efficient means of total control in appropriate establishments.

Other publications in this series

(Given below are details of all Health Technical Memoranda available from HMSO. HTMs marked (*) are currently being revised, those marked (†) are out of print. Some HTMs in preparation at the time of publication of this HTM are also listed).

1   Anti-static precautions: rubber, plastics and fabrics*†
2   Anti-static precautions: flooring in anaesthetising areas (and data processing rooms)*, 1977.
3   –
4   –
5   Steam boiler plant instrumentation†
6   Protection of condensate systems: filming amines†
2007   Electrical services: supply and distribution, 1993.
8   –
9   –
2010   Sterilization, 1994.
2011   Emergency electrical services, 1993.
12   –
13   –
2014   Abatement of electrical interference, 1993.
16   –
17   Health building engineering installations: commissioning and associated activities, 1978.
18   Facsimile telegraphy: possible applications in DGHs†
19   Facsimile telegraphy: the transmission of pathology reports within a hospital – a case study†
2020   Electrical safety code for low voltage systems, 1993.
2021   Electrical safety code for high voltage systems, 1993.
2022   Medical gas pipeline systems, 1994.
23   Access and accommodation for engineering services†
24   –
2025   Ventilation in healthcare premises, 1994.
26   Commissioning of oil, gas and dual fired boilers: with notes on design, operation and maintenance†
27   Cold water supply storage and mains distribution* [Revised version will deal with water storage and distribution], 1978.
28 to 39 –
2040   The control of legionellae in healthcare premises – a code of practice, 1993.
41 to 49 –
2050   Risk management in the NHS estate, 1994.
51 to 54 –
2055   Telecommunications (telephone exchanges), 1994.

Component Data Base (HTMs 54 to 70)

54.1   User manual, 1993.
55   Windows, 1989.
56   Partitions, 1989.
57   Internal glazing, 1989.
58   Internal doorsets, 1989.
59   Ironmongery, 1989.
60   Ceilings, 1989.
61   Flooring, 1989.
62   Demountable storage systems, 1989.
63   Fitted storage systems, 1989.
64   Sanitary assemblies, 1989.
65   Signs†
66   Cubicle curtain track, 1989.
67   Laboratory fitting-out system, 1993.
68   Ducts and panel assemblies, 1993.
69   Protection, 1993.
70   Fixings, 1993.
71 to 80 –

Firecode

81   Firecode: fire precautions in new hospitals, 1987.
81   Supp 1, 1993.
82   Firecode: alarm and detection systems, 1989.
83   Fire safety in healthcare premises: general fire precautions, 1994.
85   Firecode: fire precautions in existing hospitals, 1994.
86   Firecode: fire risk assessment in hospitals, 1994.
87   Firecode: textiles and furniture, 1993.
88   Fire safety in health care premises: guide to fire precautions in NHS housing in the community for mentally handicapped/ill people, 1986.

New HTMs in preparation

Lifts
Washers for sterile production

Health Technical Memoranda published by HMSO can be purchased from HMSO bookshops in London (post orders to PO Box 276, SW8 5DT), Edinburgh, Belfast, Manchester, Birmingham and Bristol or through good booksellers. HMSO provide a copy service for publications which are out of print; and a standing order service.

Enquiries about Health Technical Memoranda (but not orders) should be addressed to: NHS Estates, Department of Health, Marketing and Publications Unit, 1 Trevelyan Square, Boar Lane, Leeds LS1 6AE.

About NHS Estates

NHS Estates is an Executive Agency of the Department of Health and is involved with all aspects of health estate management, development and maintenance. The Agency has a dynamic fund of knowledge which it has acquired during 30 years of working in the field. Using this knowledge NHS Estates has developed products which are unique in range and depth. These are described below.

NHS Estates also makes its experience available to the field through its consultancy services.

Enquiries should be addressed to: NHS Estates, Department of Health, 1 Trevelyan Square, Boar Lane, Leeds LS1 6AE. Tel: 0532 547000.

Some other NHS Estates products

Activity DataBase – a computerised system for defining the activities which have to be accommodated in spaces within health buildings. *NHS Estates*

Design Guides – complementary to Health Building Notes, Design Guides provide advice for planners and designers about subjects not appropriate to the Health Building Notes series. *HMSO*

Estatecode – user manual for managing a health estate. Includes a recommended methodology for property appraisal and provides a basis for integration of the estate into corporate business planning. *HMSO*

Capricode – a framework for the efficient management of capital projects from inception to completion. *HMSO*

Concode – outlines proven methods of selecting contracts and commissioning consultants. Reflects official policy on contract procedures. *HMSO*

Works Information Management System – a computerised information system for estate management tasks, enabling tangible assets to be put into the context of servicing requirements. *NHS Estates*

Health Building Notes – advice for project teams procuring new buildings and adapting or extending existing buildings. *HMSO*

Health Facilities Notes – debate current and topical issues of concern across all areas of healthcare provision. *HMSO*

Health Guidance Notes – an occasional series of publications which respond to changes in Department of Health policy or reflect changing NHS operational management. Each deals with a specific topic and is complementary to a related Health Technical Memorandum. *HMSO*

Encode – shows how to plan and implement a policy of energy efficiency in a building. *HMSO*

Firecode – for policy, technical guidance and specialist aspects of fire precautions. *HMSO*

Concise – software support for managing the capital programme. Compatible with Capricode. *NHS Estates*

Model Engineering Specifications – comprehensive advice used in briefing consultants, contractors and suppliers of healthcare engineering services to meet Departmental policy and best practice guidance. *NHS Estates*

Items noted "HMSO" can be purchased from HMSO Bookshops in London (post orders to PO Box 276, SW8 5DT), Edinburgh, Belfast, Manchester, Birmingham and Bristol or through good booksellers. Details of their standing order service are given at the front of this publication.

Enquiries about NHS Estates should be addressed to: NHS Estates, Marketing and Publications Unit, Department of Health, 1 Trevelyan Square, Boar Lane, Leeds LS1 6AE.

NHS Estates consultancy service

Designed to meet a range of needs from advice on the oversight of estates management functions to a much fuller collaboration for particularly innovative or exemplary projects.

Enquiries should be addressed to: NHS Estates Consultancy Service (address as above).

Printed in the United Kingdom for HMSO
Dd 296835   C13   3/94